A Protestant Critique of the Contraception Debate

By Austin Tallman

Questions may be directed to:
contact@TallmanPublications.com

Print ISBN: 978-0-9897604-0-9

eBook ISBN: 978-0-9897604-1-6

Contents

Introduction

I would like to begin by saying that I have nothing less than the utmost respect for those I disagree with. Those who believe that contraception is immoral are not by any means intending to do wrong, and they are indeed avoiding immoral pitfalls. However, this short book will seek to argue that while a certain practice may be permissible under God's teachings, it does not automatically become God's law.

Although this text is written as a critique of beliefs that have been historically associated with Catholics (and Protestants before the 20th century), I do not intend it to be a personal attack on Catholics or Catholicism. I will at times address my views in a direct manner, but this must not be misconstrued as ill will towards Catholics or other denominations of Christianity which prohibit contraception use. In addition, although I disagree with the Catholic position on the morality of non-abortive artificial contraception, I owe a great deal of gratitude to my Catholic friends and acquaintances. Without their perspective, I would not have taken the time to give this issue the research and contemplation it deserves.

Chapter 1

The Fundamental Problems in the Contraception Debate

The issue of contraception is a controversial one, even within Protestant denominations of Christianity. The group of Christians most well-known for opposing artificial birth control is the Catholics. If you approach your Catholic friends today about this issue, you may get different answers, depending on whether they are truly a traditional Catholic, or a more socially progressive Catholic. For the sake of argument, from here on out when I say "Catholics," I am referring to the more traditional Catholics who remain adherent to the teachings of their church.

The Catholic Church teaches that artificial contraception is morally wrong, and it has been condemned for centuries by the Catholic Church fathers, as well as many Protestant reformers. Protestants today often have trouble when discussing this with their Catholic counterparts, for two reasons I believe. First, there is a fundamental difference between Catholic and Evangelical Protestant churches which is often overlooked, and that is the issue of church authority. Catholics are accustomed to a faith that involves a great amount of church authority, and this would include the Churches' prohibition of contraception use. The Catholics see God as working through the church officials to accomplish His will. Many Protestant faiths on the other hand view God as the direct authority over them, and therefore have a difficult time grasping religious ideas that do not come directly from The Bible. This fundamental difference between the two church structures will place an enormous obstacle in front of attempts to reconcile the view on contraception. In my opinion, these viewpoints have such a large gap between them that Protestants and Catholics cannot possibly come to an agreement on the issue of contraception without reconciliation of these fundamental differences.

The second problem faced by Protestants discussing this with Catholics, in my opinion, is that many Catholics are not bringing the proper argument to the conversation. This is not an assault on the Catholic doctrine, but rather a criticism of Catholics that cannot make a case for why the use of contraception is morally wrong. However, this is not to say that many modern Catholics do not have something to say in opposition of birth control. They do, but in my opinion it is logically inconsistent. As an example, often times when a

Catholic is approached about the use of contraception, they assert that it is morally wrong, and then proceed to make an argument about why the hormonal birth control pill is bad for your health. This is not a moral argument, it is a practical argument. Whenever I fly on an airplane, I assume a certain degree of risk to my health and life, but this does not automatically make flying in an airplane morally detestable. If you base the majority of your argument against contraception on the negative health effects of the birth control pill, you are going to be left speechless when someone suggests using a barrier method instead.

Often times my Catholic counterparts will try to bring "scientific studies" into the argument to prove to me that the hormonal birth control pill is bad for women's health. I object to this, even if these studies are correct, because it is not directly related to the morality of contraception. After all, there are many forms of birth control that do not affect hormones, and therefore this is an irrelevant point to make. Furthermore, if I were a Catholic, I would be extremely embarrassed if people from my church were trying to make an argument this way. I would strongly advocate for the discontinuation of citing scientific studies. This is because anyone can say that "they" discovered X in some study, and try to rely on this to win an argument. This is extremely lazy intellectual argumentation, and you do not need to cite scientific studies in order to prove a moral point if there is logical reasoning to vindicate your beliefs. When you read the bible, you never hear Jesus say anything along the lines of: "Actually, there is a new study out of Jerusalem that proves sinning is bad for your health..."

In addition, science is always changing, and at any given time, there will always be a new study that proves either side of an argument. A basic online search for "health benefits of the birth control pill" will bring up studies involving thousands of women and lower instances of death. Whether these studies are right or wrong is irrelevant, there is plenty of credible scientific evidence to prove either side of the argument concerning the hormonal birth control pill and health. If you try to make the argument on one side of the scientific evidence, your opponents will obviously cling to the opposing evidence and nobody wins. When Catholics try to bring scientific studies into the contraception debate, they are dooming themselves to failure.

My criticism thus far does not even take into account the fact that the Catholic Church fathers made an argument against contraception without statistical data on medications. It would be my recommendation that Catholics dedicate themselves to careful study of the Catholic Church fathers, if that is what their faith prescribes. Not only will this study enrich them with a better understanding of their beliefs and their ability to argue them, but it will also strengthen their faith. As soon as I hear a Catholic say the words: "studies have shown," I immediately know that they have no idea why they believe what they believe.

A thorough understanding of this moral argument is an important responsibility for both Catholics and Protestants. A well written formal explanation of the Catholic position on birth control was released by Pope Paul VI in his 1968 encyclical Humanae Vitae. I would highly recommend reading this, no matter what denomination of Christianity you belong to. Although I fundamentally disagree with some of the positions taken in Humanae Vitae, it is a beautiful work, and it will be quoted several times throughout this text.

Chapter 2

The Two Sides of the Debate

In this chapter, we will examine some of the most common arguments both for and against the morality of contraception. Each argument is numerically organized by topic.

[1] Scientific Studies

The most common reasoning brought to the table when I discuss the topic of contraception with Catholic counterparts is the argument of health dangers based on scientific studies. Given our discussion in the previous chapter, it is my hope that this argument is no longer considered acceptable. With this assumption, we will move on to other arguments.

[2] Is Contraception Murder Before Conception?

There are some individuals within the Christian community who view the act of contraception as essentially murdering an un-conceived life. It is believed that they do not have the right to deny life when God wills it, and thus they believe in being open to having as many children as God wants. There are various Protestant groups and some Catholic individuals who hold this view, although it is a minority opinion among Protestants and Catholics alike. As we will see later, even Catholic Popes acknowledge it is sometimes necessary to space births, and thus Catholic teaching opposes this belief. Upon examination of the topic, it should become readily apparent that this belief is completely illogical.

This radical belief is held by some who see it as wrong to block any opportunity to procreate. These individuals take things one step too far by proclaiming that contraception or abstinence during marriage would be denying life to a human not yet conceived. According to their interpretation of Christianity, because children are a gift from God, it would be wrong to do anything to prevent receiving the gift of another child. Some take this even further and compare the act of contraception to murder since you are denying life to a potential person.

To those who say that not having children is essentially murder before conception, this is ludicrous. Does it not say in the bible that it is good not to marry if you can do so? (1 Corinthians 7: 8, 32-35) People who adhere to this belief are creating a moral obligation to procreate, and every missed opportunity is murder. By this logic, priests practicing celibacy are sinful. We must also ask why did Jesus not have children. In addition, you will have to require that people get married when they are prepubescent so that they can begin reproducing as much as possible as soon as they are able, lest they miss an opportunity to procreate and thus deny life. If you believe that not conceiving is somehow denying life, you are going to have to open the door to all sorts of un-biblical and bizarre obligations/regulations.

Furthermore, children are one of the most wonderful gifts from God, but this does not mean that we cannot take measures to control the amount or timing of our gifts. Isn't food a gift from God, particularly chocolate? Just because I have access to chocolate, that doesn't mean I must consume as much as I possibly can in order to prevent myself from rejecting a gift from God. God does not want me to become sick and sacrifice my health just because I don't want to refuse any opportunities for

His gifts; He gives us the ability to reason and make appropriate choices.

[3] Biblical Arguments

In this section, I would like to address the only biblical passage I have seen used as a support for the argument against birth control. We find this in Genesis:

"Then Judah said to Onan, "Go in to your brother's wife and perform the duty of a brother-in-law to her, and raise up offspring for your brother." But Onan knew that the offspring would not be his. So whenever he went in to his brother's wife he would waste the semen on the ground, so as not to give offspring to his brother. And what he did was wicked in the sight of the Lord, and he put him to death also." (Genesis 38:8-10 ESV)

This passage certainly raises some questions, but it is all too often interpreted incorrectly. Perhaps an analogy followed by discussion will make the interpretation clear.

Say, for example, that Onan is working in a hospital. He is given a syringe full of medicine that must be administered to a sick patient in order for that patient to live. It is his duty by law to keep that patient alive. Onan takes the syringe over to the patient and proceeds to dump the medicine on the floor. He then returns with the empty syringe and turns it in to his supervisor. The patient dies, and it is discovered what Onan did. Onan is sentenced to the death penalty and dies. Now, why was Onan sentenced to death? Was Onan killed because of the fact he dumped medicine on the floor? Perhaps he was killed because of his implicit intent on abandoning his legal obligations and killing a patient. In a literal and explicit sense, did he dump medicine on the floor? Yes, but that isn't the real evil here.

Returning now to the actual passage at hand, we must look for the full meaning in this quote. Did God kill Onan for spilling his seed, or were there impure motives behind this act that got Onan struck down? It is commonly understood that Onan made this effort to avoid impregnating his brother's wife for selfish reasons. He wanted to experience the pleasure from sex, but he did not want to fulfill his obligation for his brother, and he did not want a child that was not his own, likely out of pride and reluctance to lose a portion of his potential inheritance. We must also pay attention to the fact that this passage clearly says that it was his duty to provide offspring for his brother, and by avoiding impregnation, he is not fulfilling an obligation under

16

the law. It is clear to me that Onan was struck down because of his purely selfish actions and not the explicit outward manifestations of this. However, this scripture is a wonderful reminder that even if contraception is permissible, it could be abused for selfish and impure reasons, and therefore could be used as an instrument of sin.

We must also consider the fact that if people want to adhere to this at face value as standing law, then they are going to have to require that a brother-in-law impregnates his brother's wife as he would his own if his brother dies. Going back to Old Testament law is sure to get some publicity. Thankfully, I believe we can agree this is not to be enforced at one hundred percent face value.

[4] Threefold Intercourse

The Catholic Church believes that intercourse is threefold, and it must satisfy all of the following to be moral: marital, unitive, and procreative. Again, we have reached the difficult issue of church authority. When this argument arises, the common Protestant question is where in the bible do these three requirements come from, specifically the procreative requirement? This threefold requirement is not explicitly in the bible, but rather comes from the work of church fathers and moral philosophers. When pressing a Catholic counterpart on the origins of these three requirements, you will eventually get to the point where they admit it comes from human thought, and not directly from the bible. From the Evangelical Protestant perspective, we are going to follow the bible, and proclamations of God's law that do not come directly from God, but rather are constructed by human beings, are subject to the fallen nature of humanity. On the other hand, it is the Catholic belief that God inspired the teachings of those church fathers, and therefore it is not human thought, but rather God working through them. On this point, there is no way to reconcile, Catholics believe in the authority of church teachings, and many Protestant denominations only believe in direct interpretations of the bible.

While it is biblically accurate to say that intercourse between a man and woman must be within the bounds of marriage, and this is presumably unitive, it would be inaccurate to say that it must always be procreative. Some assert that sex must always be strictly procreative due to "natural law," which is a philosophy that deduces moral rules by examining human nature. This form of logic explains that God created the sex act specifically for procreation, and the benefits of pleasure and unity are added bonuses. If this is the case, then a woman who has gone through menopause can no longer make love to her husband, because it is a known fact that she can no longer conceive a child. If a man or woman is understood to be sterile, would it not be a sin for them to make love with their spouse according to this belief? You cannot reason that moral rules change depending on your age and the functioning of your body. Considering the Ten Commandments, does God provide a list of exemptions to those rules? Moreover, a woman is generally fertile for approximately 5-6 days per month, and if intercourse must always involve procreation, then every married couple is morally responsible for accurately predicting her fertile days and only engaging in intercourse on those days with the explicit intent of procreation. If they did so on other days of the month, this would be morally wrong according to the natural law philosophy interpreted this way. If God is just, and this was His intention, one must wonder how He expected early generations to fully understand the female fertility cycle and be able to forecast it, an often daunting task even with the knowledge we have in modern times.

I agree that morally, intercourse must be within the bounds of marriage, and I agree that it should be unitive, not becoming a mere idol for pleasure, but I cannot fathom a requirement for procreation. Just because procreation can be a result of intercourse, that does not make it a requirement. If procreation is a requirement for sex to be complete, then failing to become pregnant after intercourse takes away the validity of the prior act. (By this logic, a husband and wife who make love together within marriage will have to wait for pregnancy test results before knowing whether the act was morally complete or not.)

However, the Catholic Church is not quite as strict as the possible situation discussed thus far, as Pope Paul VI states in Humanae Vitae:

"It does not, moreover, cease to be legitimate even when, for reasons independent of their will, it is foreseen to be infertile. For its natural adaptation to the expression and strengthening of the union of husband and wife is not thereby suppressed. The fact is, as experience shows, that new life is not the result of each and every act of sexual intercourse. God has wisely ordered laws of nature and the incidence of fertility in such a way that successive births are already naturally spaced through the inherent operation of these laws. The Church, nevertheless, in urging men to the observance of the precepts of the natural law, which it interprets by its constant doctrine, teaches that each and every marital act must of necessity retain its intrinsic relationship to the procreation of human life."[1]

In this encyclical, the Pope has reaffirmed that marital intercourse must "retain its intrinsic relationship to the procreation of human life," but it is still a valid act even if conception does not occur, so long as this is "independent of their will." This is somewhat contradictory. It is true that marital relations are not always procreative due to the natural fertility cycles, but engaging in intercourse while the wife is not fertile during her cycle would clearly be removing the procreative aspect of intimacy. Is this not establishing a requirement to only engage in intimacy when it is believed both man and wife are fertile, so long as you are able to do so?

Furthermore, the natural law conclusion that sex must involve procreation is much better understood as a secular philosophy argument, and not as a Christian understanding that is biblical. An evolutionary moral philosopher, who views human beings as intellectually evolved biological organisms, could easily come to the conclusion that intercourse is intrinsically for the purpose of procreation. After all, his world view is that we are simply organisms that must reproduce, and the pleasure and positive emotions that come along with this are just biological motivators to sustain the race.

On the other side of the coin, we have Christianity, which purports that human beings have a spirit, and that we are spiritual creatures. Perhaps there is a spiritual element to sexual relations, as opposed to only looking at the biological functions of the human body when deciding moral rules. In my view, these natural law ideals are simply creations of secular philosophy, based on biology, somehow tied into Christianity. You can come to these same conclusions under the premise of there being no God, if the idea is given due reverence.

The bible provides evidence that the relations between a man and woman within marriage are in fact more than a biological function. The following verses discuss the joy man experiences in loving his wife and enjoying her beauty: "Let your fountain be blessed, and rejoice in the wife of your youth, a lovely deer, a graceful doe. Let her breasts fill you at all times with delight; be intoxicated always in her love." (Proverbs 5:18, 19 ESV) Perhaps intercourse between a husband and wife can serve more than one purpose, purposes being both biological and spiritual. If God created intercourse that must always be open to procreation, then why is the pleasure and unity between man and wife that comes from sex still possible even if they are infertile?

However, a distinction must be made here. Pope Paul VI's teachings in Humanae Vitae clarify that the modern Catholic position on procreation in marital intercourse can be better interpreted as an obligation to being open to the possibility of pregnancy. This opens the door to what is referred to as "Natural Family Planning," while still adhering to a no artificial contraception rule. This brings us to our next topic of discussion.

[5] Natural Family Planning (NFP)

Natural family planning, often abbreviated (NFP), is the solution to not using artificial contraception, according to The Catholic Church. It involves different methods of monitoring fertility based on the woman's menstrual cycle in an effort to avoid conception. The Catholic Church advocates the use of NFP only in special circumstances when a pregnancy would legitimately be a problem, such as a period of financial distress. The following is what Pope Paul VI has to say about NFP in Humanae Vitae:

"If therefore there are well-grounded reasons for spacing births, arising from the physical or psychological condition of husband or wife, or from external circumstances, the Church teaches that married people may then take advantage of the natural cycles immanent in the reproductive system and engage in marital intercourse only during those times that are infertile, thus controlling birth in a way which does not in the least offend the moral principles which We have just explained...

Neither the Church nor her doctrine is inconsistent when she considers it lawful for married people to take advantage of the infertile period but condemns as always unlawful the use of means which directly prevent conception, even when the reasons given for the later practice may appear to be upright and serious. In reality, these two cases are completely different. In the former the married couple rightly use a faculty provided them by nature. In the later they obstruct the natural development of the generative process. It cannot be denied that in each case the married couple, for acceptable reasons, are both perfectly clear in their intention to avoid children and wish to make sure that none will result. But it is equally true that it is exclusively in the former case that husband and wife are ready to abstain from intercourse during the fertile period as often as for reasonable motives the birth of another child is not desirable. And when the infertile period recurs, they use their married intimacy to express their mutual love and safeguard their fidelity toward one another. In doing this they certainly give proof of a true and authentic love."[1]

Later, Pope John Paul II also commented on this:

"When there is a reason not to procreate, this choice is permissible and may even be necessary. However, there remains the duty of carrying it out with criteria and methods that respect the total truth of the marital act in its unitive and procreative dimension, as wisely regulated by nature itself in its biological rhythms. One can comply with them and use them to advantage, but they cannot be "violated" by artificial interference."[2]

I must respectfully disagree with what the Popes have said here. Given the following verses from the bible, it is clear that husband and wife should not be abstaining from intimacy, with the only exception to this being for the purpose of devoting themselves to prayer. In order to effectively practice NFP, it may be necessary to abstain from intimacy longer than desirable for the couple.

"The husband should give to his wife her conjugal rights, and likewise the wife to her husband. For the wife does not have authority over her own body, but the husband does. Likewise the husband does not have authority over his own body, but the wife does. Do not deprive one another, except perhaps by agreement for a limited time, that you may devote yourselves to prayer; but then come together again, so that Satan may not tempt you because of your lack of self-control." (1 Corinthians 7:3-5 ESV)

If you look into the use of natural family planning, its advocates tout that it is the way to go because it is natural, more open to life than contraceptives, strengthening for the marriage, and it is also just as effective as "the pill." I should add that when people say NFP is just as effective as the pill, this is assuming perfect practice of the method. Typical use of NFP actually carries a failure rate of around 24% per year.[3-4] For the sake of argument, though, I will assume NFP is being practiced perfectly. After researching this topic extensively, I have no doubt that NFP can be a good thing for some couples, and that it is a healthier choice for the woman compared to hormonal contraceptives. However, I see several detrimental flaws in the modern advocacy of it.

When people make an argument for the use of NFP, they will almost certainly try to convince you partly on the basis that NFP is just as effective as the pill when it is practiced correctly. This is where we first run into some deep problems. Up until now, there has been emphatic objection to the idea of removing the procreative aspect of intercourse, but now all of a sudden it is permitted under certain circumstances. The use of NFP takes the "fertility" aspect out of the threefold requirement for intercourse the Catholic's subscribe to, and therefore I cannot understand how NFP is permissible in the

Catholic Church under any circumstances. This violates their basic Church doctrine. The Catholics should be horrified by the idea of NFP, lest they want to contradict themselves.

In my opinion, the approval of NFP undermines the entire Catholic argument against the use of contraception. By allowing people to use NFP, you are ultimately admitting that God does give his people the ability to make prudent decisions about timing the birth of our children by taking steps to control fertility, without indifferently surrendering ourselves to His will. The argument then comes down to the means by which we take on that responsibility, and the Catholics often believe the objective is "being more open to life."

Proponents of NFP assert that it is just as effective as regular contraception, yet it is more "open" to life. On the surface, these statements are utterly illogical. If we are comparing two bullet shields, and we are certain that they are both 99 % accurate at blocking bullets, how can we say that one blocks fewer bullets than the other? When comparing two methods of regulating pregnancy, if they are both equally effective, how is one more "open" to life than the other? Wouldn't NFP have to be less effective than other methods at preventing pregnancy? In practice, it is my understanding that the NFP proponents are saying that artificial contraception is less open to life because you are actively intervening in bodily processes to prevent pregnancy. It isn't so much about the effectiveness of preventing pregnancy as it is your attitude towards it and your means of doing so. I understand where this belief is coming from, but there are certain things to consider before we condemn artificial contraception.

To believe that actively intervening in biological processes with artificial means is less open to life than NFP in every case would be inaccurate. With NFP, you are still intervening in your biological functions, but you are doing so by modifying your behavior. If you were not intervening in your biology, then there would be no need to monitor physical signs of the wife's menstrual cycle. However, NFP usually involves detailed charting and record keeping of bodily functions. This is clearly controlling your fertility through biological science. Some people say that artificial contraception is bad because you are proactively doing something to prevent pregnancy; you are taking fertility out of the act of intercourse. However, NFP does exactly the same thing; it strategically avoids pregnancy and takes fertility out of the act of intercourse. NFP and artificial contraception both accomplish the same task of avoiding pregnancy with identical accuracy. So, how can you logically say that one thing is more or less moral than another item of identical function?

This brings us to the subject of intention. There is the belief that the use of artificial contraception is inherently a sign of sinful intentions or attitudes, whereas NFP is not, although the two are identical in function. Perhaps there are some false associations within this mindset, and we can reason our way through this.

Is it possible for our actions to represent something different than the attitude in our hearts? Isn't it possible that a Catholic couple may be "open to life" in action by practicing NFP, while being un-open to life in their hearts, viewing additional children as a burden to a growing financial portfolio? Is it is possible for a devout Protestant couple to use artificial contraception, while still completely surrendering themselves to God's will, being prepared to open their lives to a child, should God bless them with one despite being on birth control? The people who say that NFP is somehow "more open to life" are making the assumption that the use of artificial contraception is somehow directly connected to your moral intentions and your faith. This is a presumptuous and fallacious error. If we have two methods that actively work to achieve the same end with equal accuracy, I agree that it is your intent behind its use that matters, but it is blatantly wrong to tie a specific method to intentions. If artificial contraception is inherently wrong because it removes fertility from marital relations, then NFP is just as guilty. I am not going to deny that people will often use artificial contraception for selfish reasons, but let us not forget that NFP could be used for the wrong reasons as well. It is my opinion that non-abortive contraception and NFP are not assigned varying degrees of morality, but that they are both amoral - having the ability to be used for either moral or immoral purposes.

The approval of using NFP to regulate the timing of our pregnancies largely boils this argument down to whether or not it is okay to employ the use of the unnatural. This brings us to our sixth topic, considerations on the morality of artificial creations.

[6] Is Something Unnatural Bad?

A common argument against birth control is: "artificial contraception is unnatural." Sure, artificial contraception does not come from nature, but neither do many life saving medications. Is it immoral to administer medication to a person having a heart attack because that medication is not natural? I once asked this question, and I received a logical response that yes, administering medication to someone with a medical problem is acceptable because this is aiding an effort to bring them back to what is natural, not lead them away. This was a good retort, but there are many other examples that do accurately make the point I originally intended. Is deodorant natural? Is shaving natural? Both of these things are unnatural, and they take human beings away from their natural condition. So, do Catholics run around hairy and smelling of body odor? All of the Catholics I know are not hairy or stinky, but perhaps they are just rebellious, and I wonder if they fear they will have to spend a great deal of time in purgatory or hell because they engaged in so much unnatural behavior.

Another thing to consider would be the fact that under these rules, an epidural during childbirth would be immoral. Taking away the pain of childbirth with artificial medicine is not natural, and even the bible says that women will endure pain during childbirth as punishment for our original sin. Wouldn't the pursuit of relieving the pain of childbirth be circumventing the will of God according to this logic? However, you do not see Catholic leaders fighting against modern medicine on the basis that epidurals are unnatural and thus inherently sinful.

Artificial creations of mankind are not inherently evil, they are amoral. It would be wrong to condemn the use of artificial contraception as evil solely because it is artificial. If God wanted us to remain in a completely "natural" state, he would not have given us the higher reasoning skills that we have. God has separated us from the animals and put us above them. You do not see animals creating artificial medicines and developing steel production facilities in order to build cities, and that is because God intended for them to live in a state of nature. On the contrary, God gave human beings the intellect we have in order for us to create and use our tools to better lives and grow the kingdom of God.

There is a clear distinction; God gave human beings the ability to create, but not the animals. If using the artificial is wrong, then you must reject the use of modern medicine, you must reject the building of cities made from artificially constructed materials, and you must then live in a state of nature without innovation and lower yourself to the level of an animal. But God did not intend for you to be at that level, He intended for you to be above it, as we read in Genesis:

"So God created man in his own image, in the image of God he created him; male and female he created them. And God blessed them. And God said to them, "Be fruitful and multiply and fill the earth and subdue it, and have dominion over the fish of the sea and over the birds of the heavens and over every living thing that moves on the earth." (Genesis 1:27, 28 ESV)

This verse clearly illustrates God's plan for mankind in creation. It explicitly places humans in an authoritative position to rule over nature.

Some individuals will accept that God does give us the ability to use our intellect to create artificial instruments for upright purposes in life, but they object to including anything artificial within marital intercourse. This is because many view intimacy between and man and wife as a spiritual, almost sacramental act, although it is not directly considered a sacrament. I agree that marital intimacy is a spiritual act, but that fact does not automatically deem that it must inherently exclude anything artificial. Protestants and Catholics alike consider The Lord's Supper to be a sacrament, and we will examine it as an example:

"Now as they were eating, Jesus took bread, and after blessing it broke it and gave it to the disciples, and said, "Take, eat; this is my body." And he took a cup, and when he had given thanks he gave it to them, saying, "Drink of it, all of you, for this is my blood of the covenant, which is poured out for many for the forgiveness of sins." (Matthew 26:26-28 ESV)

These verses detail the first Lord's Supper, orchestrated by Jesus himself. Notice that even in the time of Jesus, this act was not exclusive of everything artificial. Bread is not entirely natural, you cannot pick a loaf of bread from a tree, it must be processed and created by man through baking. Furthermore, Jesus picked up a "cup" and instructed the disciples to drink from it. A cup is by all means an artificial creation of man. If anyone believes that artificial creations must not be involved in spiritual acts, I am eager to see them try to partake in The Lord's Supper without the use of anything artificial. This would even be contrary to the way Jesus originated it.

Artificial, inanimate creations are amoral, being of use for moral or immoral purposes. Guns can be used to hunt animals for feeding orphans, or they can be used for the unjust killing of people, aspirin can be taken to relieve a headache or other medical malady, or it could be used in excessive doses to poison someone, and artificial contraception could be used for eliminating the consequences of infidelity, or it could be used for prudent family planning in a Christian home.

Chapter 3
Medical Aspects of Contraception with Moral Implications

When a Christian couple decides to use contraception for moral reasons, it is important to have an acute understanding of the type of contraception selected, and the moral implications of its use. There is a critical distinction to be made here, and that is that even if there are morally unacceptable forms of birth control, that does not automatically make the act of contraception altogether immoral. Furthermore, although I expressed a deep rejection of bringing scientific studies into the debate over the morality of the act of contraception, that does not mean that science cannot be useful in guiding our execution of an act which we know to be morally acceptable. Scientific studies cannot be used to decide what act is a sin and what act is not a sin, but science can be used to better our understanding of worldly objects, some of which may result in sin if used in a certain way.

In this third chapter, we will briefly examine various types of contraception, and consider the moral implications of their use. In order to ensure a complete understanding of the way many pharmaceutical types of contraception work, I will provide a review of the biological intricacies of procreation.

The healthy female of reproductive age will go through a single menstrual cycle once every 28 days on average. As she enters the fertile period of her cycle, her ovaries prepare to release an unfertilized egg carrying half of the DNA necessary to create a new person. When the woman ovulates, the egg is released into her fallopian tube where it awaits a sperm cell to fertilize it. If she has engaged in intercourse without the use of contraceptives, the male's sperm will travel up to the fallopian tubes. If a sperm cell and egg meet, the egg will be penetrated by the sperm and DNA will be combined. The egg is thereby fertilized.

Although the embryo (fertilized egg) will spend a few days traveling through the fallopian tube, cells are already multiplying and the small child is growing. Once the embryo reaches the uterus, it will attempt to attach itself to the inner lining of the uterus, which is referred to as the endometrium. When the embryo implants into the endometrium, there are chemical communications that take place within the woman's body that signal she is pregnant.

This is a brief overview of the way pregnancy occurs, but it is sufficient for understanding the topics we must discuss. A question of critical importance becomes apparent when studying conception, and it plays a major role in our decision making... when does life begin? Put another way, when does conception occur? There are two common answers to this, the first being when the egg is fertilized by the sperm, and the second being when the fertilized egg implants into the endometrium.

The time at which a sperm cell fertilizes an egg has historically been considered to be the point of conception, and this is the position taken by most pro-life advocates and Christians. During the 1970's, many in the medical community began to recognize implantation into the endometrium as the point of conception. This has been considered a political move by many in the pro-life community. From a physician's perspective, the point of implantation is medically significant, as this is when a woman's body recognizes that it is pregnant. In addition, pregnancy testing is not possible until implantation has occurred, because only then will the embryonic hormone human chorionic gonadotropin (HCG) become present in the blood.

It is important to keep in mind that although a pregnancy cannot yet be detected through testing, this doesn't necessarily indicate that there is not a living child within the mother. Let us not forget that when fertilization occurs, DNA from mother and father combine together, and the cells of this tiny human begin to multiply. It is hard to deny that this growing biological union of mother and father is anything other than a living person, albeit small and not yet implanted into the uterus.

Given the belief that life begins at fertilization, we must make the distinction between what is contraceptive and what is abortifacient. If something is contraceptive, then it works by preventing the fertilization of an egg by a sperm cell, and thus it has not destroyed life, but rather prevented life from being created. On the other hand, something that is used to end life after fertilization has occurred is clearly abortifacient, and thus murder. It is crucial to understand the biological concepts at work here because, although contraception has legitimate and moral uses, abortion is understandably detestable in the eyes of The Lord.

At this time, many Christians are in a state of confusion surrounding what is contraceptive and what is abortifacient. Many others do not even realize that some contraceptives may have abortifacient properties. There is an ongoing debate as to whether or not birth control pills and other pharmaceutical contraceptives can cause abortions. I will present some information within this chapter regarding the subject, and I will provide you with my opinion on the matter. However, I highly recommend you take the time to research this for yourself, and acquire a thorough understanding of contraceptives. One of the most informative books available regarding this is Randy Alcorn's book: "Does the Birth Control Pill Cause Abortions?" In his book, Randy collects medical information from various sources pertaining to this question, and also includes guidance on the issue.

In my personal research, I have learned several things that have come as a complete surprise to me when it comes to pharmaceutical contraception. As of several months ago, I would never have suspected that birth control pills or other contraceptive products could cause abortion. I had not grown up hearing this, and whenever I heard this occasional claim, I brushed it off as an uneducated scare tactic used by people who oppose any contraceptive use. It was not until the day when I was reading through the "full prescribing information" for a contraceptive product that something caught my eye and lead me to research this further. Within the prescribing information, under the section for "mechanism of action" (explaining how the drug works), I noticed that one of the methods by which this product functioned was preventing implantation into the uterus. After reading this, I checked another medication, then another, until everything unraveled before my eyes.

If you hold the view that life begins at fertilization, the point at which a cell from mother and father meet and a child begins to grow, wouldn't the act of preventing that tiny life from attaching to the mother's uterus be abortion? After fertilization, that small child must travel to the uterus and implant in order for it to begin receiving the nutrients that enable it to survive. Do we really want to run the risk of creating life, and then hinder the ability of that child to properly attach to its mother and grow?

An understanding of pharmaceutical contraceptives is necessary in order to comply with these moral precepts. Thus, let us go through an explanation of these medicines. The typical birth control pill, injection, or hormonal IUD (Intrauterine Device), works in the following three ways: inhibition of sperm transport to the egg via thickening of cervical mucus, prevention of ovulation (release of the egg), and causing alterations to the endometrium which inhibit implantation. The first two mechanisms are generally accepted to be contraceptive in nature, due to the fact that they work to prevent sperm and egg from coming together to create life. The third method listed here, however, often referred to as the "third mechanism," is where a Christian's main concern lies. The problem we are presented with is the fact that we know in some cases all three mechanisms fail, and a pregnancy occurs. What we do not know, and what we should worry about, is how often the first two mechanisms fail, but not the third, resulting in a fertilized egg that cannot implant into the mother's uterus.

There is a lot of controversy regarding the third mechanism of contraceptives. The American Association of Pro-life Obstetricians & Gynecologists has two papers published on their website, one by a group of physicians that argue the birth control pill does not cause abortions, and another paper by a group of physicians who assert the pill does have the potential to cause early abortions. When physicians within the pro-life community cannot agree on the abortifacient nature of chemical contraceptives, we are faced with a real problem as Christians, given most of us are not reproductive specialists who can determine the truth about contraceptives. This is further complicated by the fact that there are currently no practical and ethical means available to test the nature and frequency of the potentially abortive effects of this third mechanism.

It is suggested that hormonal contraceptives alter the lining of the uterus (the endometrium); by causing it to become thinner than it normally would be during the implantation phase of the fertility cycle. If the mechanism that prevents ovulation fails, the egg is released and possibly fertilized. If the egg is then fertilized, this tiny new life travels to a uterus which is not as receptive to it as it normally would be. Some have argued, however, that this is not an issue. Because there are a small number of pregnancies that do occur while on hormonal contraceptives, and the fact that embryos sometimes implant in the wrong place (ectopic pregnancy), some are lead to believe that an embryo is capable of implanting in a uterus, even if the endometrium is not hospitable to it. As Randy Alcorn explains in his book:

"To point out a blastocyst is capable of implanting in a fallopian tube or a thinned endometrium is akin to pointing to a seed that begins to grow on asphalt or springs up on the hard dry path. Yes, the seed is thereby shown to have an invasive nature. But surely no one believes its chances of survival are as great on a thin hard rocky path as in cultivated fertilized soil."[5]

We could go on and on debating whether or not the mechanics of pharmaceutical contraceptives can prevent the implantation of an embryo, but for the purposes of this book, we will move on to the moral applications of what we know. So, what do we know? We know there is the possibility that some chemical contraceptives can cause an early abortion, if they do in fact prevent a child from implanting into the endometrium when they would have otherwise. Although this is up for debate, we cannot rule it out as a possibility. Furthermore, it is hard to ignore the fact that pharmaceutical companies which produce these medications/devices list "inhibition of implantation" as one of the ways that these contraceptives work. Even with uncertainty, can we in good conscience as Christians choose to take the risk of interfering with the development of a child we have created? If you operate a factory and it is most convenient for you to dump your chemical waste into a river, is it really moral to do this before you know for sure how this will affect people and the environment downstream?

The sad reality of this is, at the time of this book's publication, I am unaware of a single type of contraceptive pill, injection, or implant that does not have the potential for inhibiting implantation, based on the medical data for that drug/device. Often times consulting the "full prescribing information" for a contraceptive is all you need to do in order to discover that it may inhibit implantation. Probably the most common statement used to explain the mechanism of action for birth control pills is:

"Combination oral contraceptives act by suppression of gonadotropins. Although the primary mechanism of this action is inhibition of ovulation, other alterations include changes in the cervical mucus (which increase the difficulty of sperm entry into the uterus) and changes in the endometrium (which reduce the likelihood of implantation)."

This seems to be the industry standard statement, as I have seen this on multiple medical websites and within the full prescribing information for various drugs. There are some sources that word it differently though, some of which do not even explicitly mention the effects on the endometrium and implantation, but rather give an explanation using medical terminology most people will not be able to understand.

As a reference on the next page, I list the most common contraceptive chemical substances found in pills, injections, and implants alike. Beside each is a reference for one or two sources explaining the mechanism of action for that particular drug, including a statement about the effect on the endometrium. These sources can be found at the end under "references". Each drug is listed by generic chemical name, and not brand name, due to the fact there may be several trade names for a single drug or drug combination product. If you are curious about a specific brand, check the packaging to find the generic drug(s) it contains, or reference the information included with the prescription.

Norethindrone/ethinyl estradiol[6-7]
Levonorgestrel/ ethinyl estradiol[8-9]
Drospirenone/ethinyl estradiol[10-11]
Mestranol/norethindrone[12]
Ethynodiol/ethinyl estradiol[13-14]
Norgestimate/ethinyl estradiol[15-16]
Norgestrel/ethinyl estradiol[17-18]
Norethindrone[19-20]
Norelgestromin/ethinyl estradiol[21]
Desogestrel/ethinyl estradiol[22]
Etonogestrel (Implant)[23]
Etonogestrel/ethinyl estradiol (Vaginal ring)[24]
Medroxyprogesterone (Injection)[25]
Drospirenone/ethinyl estradiol/levomefolate[26]
Estradiol valerate/dienogest[27]
Estradiol and medroxyprogesterone[28]
Levonorgestrel (Emergency contraceptive)[29-30]
Ulipristal acetate (Emergency contraceptive)[31]
Levonorgestrel (IUD)[32]
Intrauterine Copper Contraceptive (IUD)[33]

It is an unfortunate fact that all of the contraceptive products listed have a medically documented potential to prevent implantation. However, it should be noted that there is growing evidence that a very controversial product may not actually pose a risk of abortion. There have been many studies and articles released recently, showing that levonorgestrel pills used as emergency contraception (the morning after pill), do not in fact prevent implantation. At this time, the drug does include the possibility of preventing implantation within its prescribing information, but several news articles indicate that drug manufacturers are currently trying to get approval to remove this from their warning labels. It is believed that this drug may act solely to delay ovulation if it has not yet occurred, while leaving the endometrium unaffected.[34]

It is also interesting to note that the Catholic bishops of Germany approved the use of "morning-after pills" for instances of rape in early 2013, holding the belief that these are acceptable, so long as they are contraceptive and not abortifacient.[35] If you would ever considering using this product, I recommend that you extensively research this topic (keeping in mind the Christian belief of when life begins), as the developments are ongoing at the time of this book's publication. I will provide links and information as well at: www.AProtestantCritique.com.

I find it quite ironic that out of the many pharmaceutical contraceptives available, the levonorgestrel morning after pill is the one product that currently has the potential to be declared a non-abortifacient, given the amount of scrutiny it has received. It is my hope that these products will be proven not to have an abortive potential, as such a product could be useful in situations such as rape, and possible prevention of unplanned pregnancies that would result in abortion. I would personally require more supporting evidence, and the removal of implantation effects from the prescribing information before using this product, but the latest information makes me hopeful. It should be noted that this new evidence applies to emergency contraception pills containing levonorgestrel only, and that there is more skepticism surrounding other regular or emergency use products.

Although the current pharmaceutical landscape surrounding contraception is grim, that does not mean that new developments will not occur in the future, which may in fact provide a medicine that prevents pregnancy (fertilization), without bearing the risk of abortion. There has been research conducted on attempting the development of a male "birth control pill," which would inhibit the release of sperm, and thus prevent fertilization without carrying the risk of abortion. Such a product is not available as of yet. Time will show us what advances in medicine will be possible.

Furthermore, we must briefly address the other common contraceptive products. These would be barrier methods (condoms, etc.) and spermicides (products that kill sperm before reaching the egg). From a moral standpoint, the use of these products is acceptable in my opinion, when used for legitimate reasons, given that they are solely contraceptive.

Spermicides are a group of chemicals that come in the form of foams, jellies, creams, suppositories, or films. These work to prevent sperm from fertilizing an egg by killing them before they can reach the uterus. There have been concerns in the past that spermicides could cause birth defects in children conceived while using the products, however, it appears that many studies over several decades have proven this is not the case.[36-37] If these products did in fact pose the risk of birth defects, they would be morally objectionable. Because spermicides work by preventing pregnancy before fertilization, they are therefore solely contraceptive in nature.

Barrier methods work by keeping sperm from entering the uterus, and thus they cannot fertilize an egg when they are used effectively. Because these methods do not allow sperm and egg to meet, they only function to prevent a pregnancy, and thus are acceptable contraceptives.

There is concern that this method of birth control can lead to a higher risk of preeclampsia in a woman who conceives a child after using barrier contraceptives.[38] Preeclampsia is a condition where a mother's body experiences high blood pressure and other systemic problems, which is potentially dangerous for the mother and child. The increased risk of preeclampsia is not directly due to the presence of a barrier birth control product, but rather the lack of exposure to the husband's sperm that results from its use. It is suggested that prolonged and repeated exposure to the husband's sperm will allow the mother's body to become used to it, and this therefore prevents any immune system responses to the presence of the foreign substance. If you use barrier methods of contraception and wish to conceive in the future, you may consider using barrier methods only during the fertile period of the wife's menstrual cycle, as this may allow her system to adapt to the presence of her husband's sperm before getting pregnant. You will need to research this and figure out what will work best for you.

Finally, there is one last aspect of contraceptive use to be considered, and that is the question of health effects. It is important to realize that the benefits or dangers to your health that arise from using contraceptives are separate from the issue of whether or not it is moral to use contraceptives. With that in mind, this does not mean that there are no moral considerations when making choices about your health. It is clear from the bible that God expects us to respect our bodies and take care of ourselves:

"Or do you not know that your body is a temple of the Holy Spirit within you, whom you have from God? You are not your own, for you were bought with a price. So glorify God in your body." (1 Corinthians 6:19, 20 ESV)

Given all that we have examined, I implore you to make wise choices about contraception that result from thorough research and contemplation. I am personally skeptical when it comes to taking non-essential medications that will have a profound impact on bodily systems. However, medicine is a complicated part of our earthly life, and I pray that we can continue to develop new and better moral methods to improve our lives and the lives of our brothers and sisters.

Chapter 4

A Protestant Critique of the
Contraception Debate

This book has allowed us to look at several
viewpoints pertaining to the issue of contraception
within the Christian community. It is important to
keep in mind the fundamental differences between
Catholicism and many Protestant denominations
when considering this, and other issues. There are
some topics, such as this one, which I do not believe
can be reconciled to a universal belief among all
Christians. With this in mind, let us remember that
although we may not be able to agree on everything,
we are all still brothers and sisters in Christ, and we
should still support each other as such.

As a Protestant, I hear a lot of people criticizing
my position on contraception, due to the fact that it
was essentially condemned by all Christians until
recent times. There are also remarks being made by
some Catholics who say that the Protestant
acceptance of contraception is the result of giving in
to the pressure of a secular society. To make this
claim is to lower yourself to a naive attempt at
mischaracterizing those who you disagree with. As

this book shows, there is a logical moral argument that opposes the idea that the use of artificial birth control is universally unacceptable.

In addition, let us not forget that the 1963-1966 papal birth control commission issued an opinion that contraception is permissible. Although this committee did not have doctrinal authority, the majority opinion was in favor of allowing the use of contraception. This report from the commission led Pope Paul VI to release his historic Humanae Vitae, which defended the ban on contraception. Furthermore, a May 2012 poll found that 82% of Catholics in the United States believe birth control is "morally acceptable," despite the fact that the church does not permit its use.[39] For those who wish to sternly criticize Protestants for allowing the use of contraception, do not forget that this issue is something widely debated even among the Catholic community.

The Catholic Church authority has come to a conclusion about contraception based on their fundamental understanding of Christianity, and many Protestants have come to a different conclusion. There is an objective right and wrong answer to this issue, but I ask all of us, as Christians, to carry on this debate respectfully.

In this final chapter, I will summarize my Protestant opinion on the issue of contraception. To begin, let's consider where we should get our information for moral issues. As I mentioned before, I strongly object to using scientific studies to try to prove a moral argument. If you attempt to do this with contraception, you are setting yourself up for trouble if a study comes out that proves some form of artificial birth control is good for your health. Instead, it is better to look to the bible for guidance. The following verses discuss the significance of scripture:

"The law of the Lord is perfect, reviving the soul; the testimony of the Lord is sure, making wise the simple; the precepts of the Lord are right, rejoicing the heart; the commandment of the Lord is pure, enlightening the eyes; the fear of the Lord is clean, enduring forever; the rules of the Lord are true, and righteous altogether." (Psalm 19:7-9 ESV)

"How sweet are your words to my taste, sweeter than honey to my mouth! Through your precepts I get understanding; therefore I hate every false way. Your word is a lamp to my feet and a light to my path." (Psalm 119:103-105 ESV)

If God's word is where "I get understanding" and "a lamp to my feet and a light to my path," then do we really need to add on to the word of God or try to perfect it? These verses make it clear to me that the word of God is sufficient, and although we rely on other men (leaders in our church), to help us understand the scripture better, that does not mean that God left the responsibility to man to determine what the law of God should be. If He intended that, then why did He give His law to Moses, and why did Jesus need to teach during His time on Earth? Because of this, I have doubts when it comes to determining what God's law is using natural law philosophy.

It is the philosophy of men that teaches that intercourse must always be procreative, and that intercourse is intended to always be simultaneously marital, unitive, and procreative. If you believe these requirements are true, then you don't believe that the bible is sufficient. The bible clearly states that sex should be marital, and it also explains that it is unitive and pleasing:

"Let marriage be held in honor among all, and let the marriage bed be undefiled, for God will judge the sexually immoral and adulterous." (Hebrews 13:4 ESV)

"Let your fountain be blessed, and rejoice in the wife of your youth, a lovely deer, a graceful doe. Let her breasts fill you at all times with delight; be intoxicated always in her love." (Proverbs 5:18, 19 ESV)

"Therefore a man shall leave his father and mother and hold fast to his wife, and the two shall become one flesh." (Ephesians 5:31 ESV)

There are several verses in the bible that explicitly support the fact that sex is intended to be unitive and within the bounds of marriage, but there is no such teaching that indicates a requirement for it to be procreative. There is nothing in the bible to be found that says a husband and wife can only make love when they intend to have children.

Some argue that the bible could not have condemned contraception because it did not exist at that time. I disagree with this. Although the bible does not tell us it is wrong to kill an innocent person with a gun, it does tell us not to murder. While the bible may not have been able to specifically refer to birth control pills, it could have given us an indication that contraception is wrong. The story of Onan cannot serve this purpose as there are plausible understandings of the story that are not a condemnation of contraception. Furthermore, if God wanted us to believe that "every act of intercourse must be open to life," or "intercourse must be marital, unitive, and procreative," then why did Jesus never say those things?

Although I do not put my faith in "natural law" teachings, if I did, I still would not agree with this conclusion. Natural law can easily justify why homosexual acts are immoral, being that they are a blatant rejection of the intended biological functions of the body. But this is not the case with contraception. On a biological level, males and females have differing anatomy with a clearly designed purpose and use. However, it would not be unnatural to separate the possibility of procreation from heterosexual intercourse, because the female is biologically designed not to be fertile at all times. She is usually only fertile for a small window of time each month, and a woman is also infertile while pregnant or after going through menopause, thus, heterosexual intercourse usually does not involve fertility. This doesn't somehow make it unnatural to have intercourse while the wife is not fertile. Intercourse that does not involve fertility could only logically be considered unnatural if both male and female were fertile 100% of the time. God is our creator and if He intended for the functions of sex to be inseparable, He could have made females fertile at all times, but He did not.

In line with Catholic principals, there are some who believe that it is wrong to withhold your fertility from your spouse. It is viewed as selfish, and in order to be a fully open and loving couple, you must not keep your fertility from your spouse when you make love. If this is true, then NFP is morally detestable. Natural Family Planning is by definition a strategic attempt to avoid having intercourse during the fertile periods of a woman's menstrual cycle. You can try to argue about NFP functioning as a different means to an end, compared to artificial contraception, but you cannot deny that this is withholding fertility, that is the entire point. Moreover, if this is true, how can you justify ever making love to your spouse if the wife is not surely fertile at the time? Pope Paul VI has acknowledged that not every act of intercourse results in pregnancy, due to the natural rhythms of a woman's body, and that is why NFP is permitted. However, it is hard to overlook a contradiction by those who believe that fertility must not be separated from intercourse, while also permitting NFP.

Of course, there are some who do in fact shy away from taking any steps to regulate the timing of births, and I object to this logic greatly. Rejecting the use of contraception and leaving it all up to God is not actually putting your faith in God, it is choosing to have as many children as possible - which you may feel you are called to do. However, this is akin to saying, "I'm not going to steer my car on the interstate, I'm just going to put my faith in God and leave it up to him to decide where to steer my car." You aren't putting your trust in God, you are choosing to likely cause a major car accident. To a certain extent, this is insulting to God, because He created you with the ability to make prudent decisions for yourself and your family. God did not intend for us to indifferently depend on Him to make every decision in life for us, He gave us the gift of intellect and free will to be able to make choices on our own.

It is also hard to deny the fact that most married couples in the world simply cannot care for a family that is as large as biologically possible. Regulating the timing of births is absolutely necessary for practical and moral reasons:

"But if anyone does not provide for his relatives, and especially for members of his household, he has denied the faith and is worse than an unbeliever." (1 Timothy 5:8 ESV)

In addition, if you believe in leaving total control up to God, you are relying on the idea that God has the power to close the wife's womb when He is content with the number of children you have. Given this belief, isn't the opposite true? If God truly wills that you have another child, is a little pill or barrier really going to be able to stop Him? If God doesn't get His will when it comes to conception, then how exactly was Jesus born of a virgin?

The last debate topic I will summarize here is the issue of whether natural contraception is superior to artificial birth control. Let me start by asking, if

God provided us with natural means to avoid pregnancy, why are artificial forms not okay as well? God provides us with water through lakes and streams, but that doesn't mean that drinking water out of pipes is somehow wrong. God provides us with caves and shade under trees for protection, but that doesn't make building a home for ourselves immoral. Some say that it is wrong to frustrate God's design of the female reproductive system. This can be resolved by using barrier contraceptive methods that do not interfere with the inner workings of the female body. Moreover, if it is immoral to interfere with God's design of our bodies, then we cannot consume anything artificial that alters the functioning of our body, such as alcohol or caffeinated beverages. This may also be grounds for declaring all high-fat, processed foods immoral.

Another problem with the artificial vs. NFP dilemma is that they achieve the same end. I obviously recognize the fact that there are countless instances where the means to an end can vary in terms of morality. A fine example would be using a barrier method of birth control that carries no risk of abortion, as opposed to different form of contraception that may also act as an abortifacient. However, when we are strictly speaking in terms of blocking conception - nothing else, then the discussion solely comes down to whether natural methods are superior to artificial ones. I personally cannot understand how something artificial is morally inferior to something natural of identical function. If Catholics believe this, then taking aspirin is immoral, because Willow Bark is a natural substance that is chemically similar and has the same effect.

It is my belief that God has blessed us with the ability to think and create, and in doing so He placed us above the animal kingdom. The fact that God gave us the ability to build and innovate is His gift to us, and in turn we can use our creations to glorify God, and improve the lives of others. It is ludicrous to believe our inventions are inherently immoral, especially when the tool is identical in function to a natural instrument provided by God.

Given the fact that many Protestant denominations accept the use of artificial birth control, let us not forget to remain vigilant when it comes to our understanding of various contraceptives. Something that particularly disturbs me is when people argue that contraceptives which prevent implantation are not a concern, because many fertilized eggs fail to implant all on their own quite frequently. However, I strongly disagree with this logic. Just because countless numbers of people will die today from natural causes, that doesn't give me the right to go out and do something that may cause the loss of someone's life. Let us not fall into

the trap of de-humanizing thinking. We have a duty
to preserve the value of a human life, and I pray that
we as Christians never forget that.

Similarly, it is important to remember to use
contraception for the right reasons. Although I
disagree with the notion that Natural Family
Planning is the only acceptable way to regulate
births, the advocates of NFP do in fact remind us of
important things to consider.

I do not agree with the idea that artificial
contraception inherently treats potential children as
a "disease" that must be prevented, it is morally
acceptable to regulate the timing of births
artificially, but we must make sure we have the right
attitude in our hearts about children and God's will.
Children are a blessing from God, and we must
rejoice if God bestows this blessing upon us, even if
we did not plan on it. Further, I don't agree that
artificial birth control will automatically demean sex
into something solely for selfish pleasure. In my
opinion, this is a matter of your heart and attitude.
Artificial contraception could be used for this
purpose, and NFP as well, but I believe we have the
ability to control ourselves, and maintain a healthy
and loving relationship with our spouse, as God
intended. A man-made tool is amoral; it can be
used for good or for evil.

Finally, it is important to realize that using
contraception is not anti-children. Nobody ever said

that having children was bad; in fact, I believe you should have as many children as you can reasonably raise - if that is what God calls you to do. Isn't raising more children to be men and women of Christ a blessing? Just because we are not "open to life" in action at a particular time when we are using contraception, that doesn't mean that we can't be open to life spiritually. We can plan the timing of our children while also completely surrendering ourselves to God's will for our life. If a couple becomes pregnant while using birth control, let them be thankful to God and rely on His divine providence to give them guidance.

I agree with Pope Paul VI when he says: "Children are really the supreme gift of marriage and contribute in the highest degree to their parents' welfare."[1] The bible also clearly talks about the beauty of having children:

"Behold, children are a heritage from the Lord, the fruit of the womb a reward. Like arrows in the hand of a warrior are the children of one's youth. Blessed is the man who fills his quiver with them! He shall not be put to shame when he speaks with his enemies in the gate." (Psalm 127:3-5 ESV)

I hope this book has been very informative for you, and I pray that the opinions I have presented here are correct. I also pray that you will ultimately seek guidance from God in the future when approaching the issue of contraception.

For more information, visit us online at:
www.AProtestantCritique.com
www.AustinTallman.com

References:

[1]Pope Paul VI. "Humanae Vitae." 25 July 1968. Web. 8 Aug 2013. <http://www.vatican.va/holy_father/paul_vi/encyclicals/documents/ hf_p-vi_enc_25071968_humanae-vitae_en.html>.

[2]John Paul II, "Parents are God's Co-workers", Sunday Angelus meditation, 17 July 1994, L'Osservatore Romano, 20 July 1994, weekly English edition 1

[3]"Effectiveness of Contraceptive Methods." . Centers for Disease Control (CDC), Web. 8 Aug 2013. <http://www.cdc.gov/reproductivehealth/UnintendedPregnancy/PD F/effectiveness_of_contraceptive_methods.pdf>.

[4]"Birth control methods fact sheet." . Office on Women's Health, U.S. Department of Health and Human Services, 21 Nov 2011. Web. 8 Aug 2013. <http://www.womenshealth.gov/publications/our-publications/fact-sheet/birth-control-methods.cfm>.

[5]Alcorn, Randy. "Does the Birth Control Pill Cause Abortions?". 10th Ed. Sandy, OR: Eternal Perspective Ministries, 2011. eBook.

[6]Oral Contraceptive Agents Description: Norethindrone and Ethinyl Estradiol Tablets. June 2006. Web. 8 Aug 2013. <http://pi.actavis.com/data_stream.asp?product_group=1205&p=pi &language=E>.

[7]Prescribing Information: norethindrone acetate and ethinyl estradiol tablets, ethinyl estradiol tablets and ferrous fumarate tablets. June 2012. Web. 8 Aug 2013. <http://www.wcrx.com/pdfs/pi/pi_loloestrinfe.pdf>.

[8]Prescribing Information: levonorgestrel / ethinyl estradiol tablets. July 2011. Web. 8 Aug 2013.

<http://dailymed.nlm.nih.gov/dailymed/lookup.cfm?setid=f1076019
-6f2c-4c90-9f3c-ab0c7cdd9315>.

[9]Prescribing Information: levonorgestrel and ethinyl estradiol. Web.
8 Aug 2013.
<http://www.accessdata.fda.gov/drugsatfda_docs/label/2008/02186
4s002lbl.pdf>.

[10]Highlights of Prescribing Information: drospirenone/ethinyl
estradiol. 10 April 2012. Web. 8 Aug 2013.
<http://labeling.bayerhealthcare.com/html/products/pi/fhc/Yasmin_
PI.pdf?WT.mc_id=www.berlex.com>.

[11]Highlights of Prescribing Information: drospirenone/ethinyl
estradiol. May 2012. Web. 8 Aug 2013.
<http://pi.actavis.com/data_stream.asp?product_group=1691&p=pi
&language=E>.

[12]ORAL CONTRACEPTIVE AGENTS DESCRIPTION:
Norethindrone and Mestranol Tablets. June 2007. Web. 8 Aug
2013.
<http://pi.actavis.com/data_stream.asp?product_group=1598&p=pi
&language=E&altp=ppi>.

[13]Prescribing Information: Ethynodiol Diacetate plus Ethinyl
Estradiol Tablets. 24 September 2003. Web. 8 Aug 2013.
<http://www.pfizer.ca/en/our_products/products/monograph/305>.

[14]Information: Ethynodiol Diacetate and Ethinyl Estradiol Tablets.
August 2006. Web. 8 Aug 2013.
<http://pi.actavis.com/data_stream.asp?product_group=1324&p=pi
&language=E&altp=ppi>.

[15]Norgestimate and ethinyl estradiol. Web. 8 Aug 2013.
<http://pi.actavis.com/data_stream.asp?product_group=1280&p=pi
&language=E&altp=ppi>.

[16]Norgestimate and ethinyl estradiol. Web. 8 Aug 2013.
<http://pi.actavis.com/data_stream.asp?product_group=1321&p=pi
&language=E&altp=ppi>.

[17]Physician Labeling: Norgestrel and Ethinyl Estradiol Tablets. July
2007. Web. 8 Aug 2013.
<http://pi.actavis.com/data_stream.asp?product_group=1292&p=pi
&language=E&altp=ppi>.

[18]Physician Labeling: Norgestrel and Ethinyl Estradiol Tablets.
Web. 8 Aug 2013.
<http://pi.actavis.com/data_stream.asp?product_group=1258&p=pi
&language=E&altp=ppi>.

[19]Prescribing Information: Norethindrone tablets. Web. 8 Aug 2013.
<http://pi.actavis.com/data_stream.asp?product_group=1252&p=pi
&language=E&altp=ppi>.

[20]Physician Labeling: Norethindrone tablets. July 2011. Web. 8 Aug
2013.
<http://pi.actavis.com/data_stream.asp?product_group=1285&p=pi
&language=E&altp=ppi>.

[21]Norelgestromin and ethinyl estradiol (Patch). June 2013. Web. 8
Aug 2013.
<http://dailymed.nlm.nih.gov/dailymed/lookup.cfm?setid=f8e8a69e
-a018-469a-af56-e20f61fe4e06>.

[22]Prescribing Information: Desogestrel and Ethinyl Estradiol
Tablets. October 2012. Web. 8 Aug 2013.
<http://pi.actavis.com/data_stream.asp?product_group=1511&p=pi
&language=E&altp=ppi>.

[23]Highlights of Prescribing Information: Etonogestrel implant. May
2012. Web. 8 Aug 2013.
<http://www.merck.com/product/usa/pi_circulars/n/nexplanon/nexp
lanon_pi.pdf>.

68

[24]Etonogestrel/ethinyl estradiol vaginal ring. May 2012. Web. 8 Aug 2013.
<http://www.merck.com/product/usa/pi_circulars/n/nuvaring/nuvaring_pi.pdf>.

[25]Highlights of Prescribing Information: Medroxyprogesterone acetate (injectable suspension), for intramuscular use. April 2012. Web. 8 Aug 2013.
<http://labeling.pfizer.com/ShowLabeling.aspx?id=522>.

[26]Highlights of Prescribing Information: drospirenone/ethinyl estradiol/levomefolate calcium tablets and levomefolate calcium tablets. April 2012. Web. 8 Aug 2013.
<http://labeling.bayerhealthcare.com/html/products/pi/fhc/Safyral_PI.pdf>.

[27]Highlights of Prescribing Information: estradiol valerate and estradiol valerate/dienogest tablets. March 2012. Web. 8 Aug 2013.
<http://labeling.bayerhealthcare.com/html/products/pi/natazia_pi.pdf>.

[28]Medroxyprogesterone acetate and estradiol cypionate injectable suspension. Web. 8 Aug 2013.
<http://www.accessdata.fda.gov/drugsatfda_docs/label/2000/20874lbl.pdf>.

[29]Pharmacist Information: Levonorgestrel. Web. 8 Aug 2013.
<http://www.levo4u.com/pdf/pharmacist_info.pdf>.

[30]Highlights of Prescribing Information: Levonorgestrel. July 2009. Web. 8 Aug 2013.
<http://www.accessdata.fda.gov/drugsatfda_docs/label/2009/021998lbl.pdf>.

[31]Highlights of Prescribing Information: ulipristal acetate tablet. April 2012. Web. 8 Aug 2013.
<http://pi.actavis.com/data_stream.asp?product_group=1699&p=pi&language=E>.

[32]Highlights of Prescribing Information: levonorgestrel-releasing intrauterine system. Feb 2013. Web. 8 Aug 2013. <http://labeling.bayerhealthcare.com/html/products/pi/Mirena_PI.pdf>.

[33]Prescribing Information: Intrauterine Copper Contraceptive. Web. 8 Aug 2013. <http://www.paragard.com/images/ParaGard_info.pdf>.

[34]Belluck, Pam. "Abortion Qualms on Morning-After Pill May Be Unfounded." New York Times 5 June 2012, Web. 8 Aug. 2013. <http://www.nytimes.com/2012/06/06/health/research/morning-after-pills-dont-block-implantation-science-suggests.html?pagewanted=all>.

[35]Brugger, E. Christian. "Does Emergency Contraception Cause Early Abortions?." National Catholic Register 25 April 2013, Web. 8 Aug. 2013. <http://www.ncregister.com/daily-news/does-emergency-contraception-cause-early-abortions>.

[36]"Fertility after contraception or abortion." PubMed.gov. National Center for Biotechnology Information, October 1990. Web. 8 Aug 2013. <http://www.ncbi.nlm.nih.gov/pubmed/2209874>.

[37]"Relationship of vaginal spermicides to birth defects." PubMed.gov. National Center for Biotechnology Information, March 1989. Web. 8 Aug 2013. <http://www.ncbi.nlm.nih.gov/pubmed/2677215>.

[38]"Barrier family planning methods as risk factor which predisposes to preeclampsia." PubMed.gov. National Center for Biotechnology Information, August 2000. Web. 8 Aug 2013. <http://www.ncbi.nlm.nih.gov/pubmed/11055107>.

[39]Newport, Frank. "Americans, Including Catholics, Say Birth Control Is Morally OK." Gallup, Inc. 22 May 2012, Web. 8 Aug. 2013. <http://www.gallup.com/poll/154799/americans-including-catholics-say-birth-control-morally.aspx>.

www.ingramcontent.com/pod-product-compliance
Lightning Source LLC
Chambersburg PA
CBHW060706030426
42337CB00017B/2781